The Geography of Kitchens

poems by

Amy Haddad

Finishing Line Press
Georgetown, Kentucky

The Geography of Kitchens

ACKNOWLEDGMENTS

Grateful acknowledgement is made to the editors and publishers of the
following periodicals in which the poems in this collection were first
published:

"An Iris Blooms in November." *Oberon Literary Journal #18*, 2021, St. James,
NY, p. 69.

"The Road to Alzheimer's Disease." *DASH Literary Journal*, 2020, 13th
Edition, p. 77.

Publisher: Leah Huete de Maines
Editor: Christen Kincaid
Cover Art and Design: Patrick Drickey
Author Photo: Steve Martin

Order online: www.finishinglinepress.com
also available on amazon.com

Author inquiries and mail orders:
Finishing Line Press
PO Box 1626
Georgetown, Kentucky 40324
USA

Table of Contents

To my maternal grandmother, Doris Marie Haring, who was one tough cookie. Her letters to my Mom, Paula Haddad, and me were the inspiration for this chapbook.

The Geography of Kitchens

The terrain of my new kitchen throws me—I open a cupboard
to get olive oil and instead find a box grater. The spatulas,
spices, mixing bowls, plates are lost to me
until the chart of the space becomes embodied, unconscious.
I hold the topography of past stoves and countertops
deep inside me. The scale of Grandma's kitchen
was so small, the refrigerator sat in its own little room
jutting out the back of the house.
The sink and cupboards divided
the entry to the dining room.
The aqua boomerang Formica table shoved
up to the window served the dual purpose
of clear space to knead dough or make noodles
then turned back into a table
where four could sit to eat or five
if one was strapped in a highchair.

My mother-in-law's kitchen had carrying capacity
for six and traded in gossip. The southern
climate was warm and steamy.
The women in the family dried dishes
with towels made from flour bags.
Like Tibetan prayer flags ragged from use,
the wet towels, embroidered with chickens
in sunbonnets and watering cans, hung
over the backs of chairs. The alluvium
from supper, potato peels and a stray pea
or two, flowed into the drain trap.
To this day, I can close my eyes, imagine
the contours of the room, reach into the drawer
to the left of her farmhouse sink
and pick out a dry towel.

Renamed

Doris Marie came first, then *Dorie.*
Too early in life she was called
Mom, Ma then *Mrs. Doris M.*
on mailing labels when she became
a young widow then *nicknames—*
Crick or *Mamie* when she looked like
Mrs. Eisenhower.
Then *Gram, Grandma* to me
Late in life she discovered her legal
name wasn't Doris but *Bessie.*
The only *Bessie* she knew
was a detested aunt on her father's
side. The date of her birth
was different too, a day later
than the date she celebrated
for eighty years. No one
left alive to ask why or when
her family changed her name to *Doris.*

Department Store Cafeteria

The cafeteria is on the lowest level
of the department store, a world of chrome
and green vinyl. I dressed up
for shopping but lunch comes first.
At six, I am tall enough to reach
the bottom shelf. We slide our trays
past tiers of salads and desserts.
My Aunt says to take what I want;
red Jell-O cubes with whipped cream
in a tulip glass. My Aunt chooses
a small bowl of cooked spinach,
another of cottage cheese—
she is on a diet. We pass ladies
in white uniforms waiting behind
clouds of steam, lacy hankies
fanned behind their name tags.
As we search for a table, I peek
at the other women eating lunch.
I know my aunt is very fashionable
because she wears button earrings,
drapes her sweater over her slim shoulders
and crosses her legs at the ankles.
She pours drops of vinegar
on her spinach, lights a cigarette.
I wonder what it means to be
"wound too tight" which is what
my mother says about my Aunt.
The acrid smell of vinegar still
summons this place and her presence,
where I sit with my Mary Janes wrapped
behind the chair legs, trying not to squirm
and watch her take tiny bites and blow
smoke above our heads.

A Spoon and a Packet of Marigold Seeds

Grandma's house, Joe's garden. He came with the house,
a bachelor boarder retired from the gypsum plant.
When Mother was a girl her older sisters teased,
said Joe wanted to marry her. His heavy footsteps
on the floorboards in his attic room woke her at night.
She panicked he might come down the stairs,
take her away. I inherited her fear.
When I was ten, I could visit Grandma alone. Took the bus
from Omaha to Fort Dodge. I avoided Joe. His garden though,
was beguiling, a green patch of longing I dared not trespass
to stay away from him. In denim head to toe,
he plodded daily in the garden, dressed the same on the hottest
and coolest days. I tracked his movements, watching
like a stray dog afraid of being kicked. Sensing my yearning,
Grandma gave me a spoon and marigold seeds,
Go plant these. He won't bite. She was right, he didn't bite, but
spit often, brown juice straight on the ground or aimed
into a rusted Folgers can. Gathering courage, I squatted at a far corner
by the radishes. I dug small holes, dropped in my seeds,
keeping track of him as he worked the rows. When he reached
the radishes he stopped, held out his hand to me, *Washdohast?*
He never spoke to me before. His accent strange, his odor strong,
I stared at him half-standing, ready to run if he tried to grab me.
He held out his hand again, pointing to the seeds.
I gave him the packet. He glanced at the seeds then waved at me
to follow to the alley-end of the garden. *Deezlikesun.*
He squinted at the sky. This sunny spot was the place
for the marigolds. That summer, I remained wary of him,
got used to his smell, never the spitting.
He showed me how to nip baby lettuce leaves
without uprooting the entire plant and tie up beans.
I learned what tending meant.

Grandma's Letters—Sweating at the Dry Cleaners

I went crazy one day and bought myself 2 new pairs of navy blue shoes—you saw one pair when you saw me last and the others are dress-uppy ones—they were on sale that day—got both pairs for $19.00. I am so thankful that I don't have any foot trouble. I can just about put on most any pair of shoes and walk out without much breaking-in. It was not always that easy.

On her feet
All day,
Sweating at the dry cleaners
Pressing shirts.

Ingrown toenails, corns, blisters,
Then it was hard
To find shoes that fit.

When to Pick Carrots

At eleven, I am old enough to be in charge
of pulling spring onions and radishes,
I choose which cucumber to pluck from the vine.
I tug on carrots whose shoulders just peek above
the soil line. I use a garden fork to sift the dirt
reveling in the magic of new potatoes. It is
amazing to me that to grow potatoes you must
plant potatoes. The earth on my hands smells
of summer and worms. I brush the excess dirt
off the carrots, lay them in a row to dry outside.
I wash my hands then the vegetables, pinch off
the green tops of the radishes and slip them into
an ice water bath. As for spring onions and cucumber,
I slice then dump them into vinegar and water,
a quick pickle counterpoint, crisp and sharp,
to my Grandma's fried chicken sizzling in lard.
The potatoes are boiled then drenched in butter.
After we eat, we sit outside in creaking metal chairs
facing the garden, listening to the moths
knock against the yellow porch light.

Grandma's Letters—The Iris Bed

*The sky today is clear. My iris bed has been a thing of beauty. Wish
I could have had a picture taken. It has never been so lovely. People
have stopped by to look and talk about it.*

Under Delft blue skies,
Frilly iris bunch and bend
Dew-heavy heads low.

Yellow-tipped tongues spark a light
On velvet, purple petals.

Hollyhock Ladies

I pulled out my tee shirt to hold the flowers
I carried back to my Aunt. A full bloom, turned upside-down
became a ruffled skirt. She pushed a short twig up
the center of the skirt and on through a just opening
flower that made the blouse, the bust dusted with pollen.
The bud was transformed into the head, topped off
by a green lacy cap. We made one hollyhock lady after another
mixing the colors until the flowers were gone. We lined
them up in a row atop the picnic table, tipsy ladies-in-waiting
wearing their best finery. Next morning, some lay scattered
about the back yard as if they took flight, others merely melted
in a heap on the table, a few lost their heads.

An Iris Blooms in November

The warmth of Indian Summer
mimics spring, confuses and teases
an iris into unfurling blue-black
petals as the weather
fast reverts to brittle
skies November gray.
Lone among the green sword
leaves, the bloom spills
the woody perfume of May
in the winter-worn garden.
I am tempted to cut it, savor
the scent a few more days
but, I choose to leave it to die
safe among the intertwined
roots where rebirth lies.

Grandma's Letters— The Kitty-Cat Clock

Well, dinner is a thing of the past, my dishes are done, and everybody has gone and left me all alone again. There is nothing on TV except repeats and I seem to have seen most everything the first time around. It's a good thing for me that I love to read and work cross word puzzles.

The fragrance of pork steak
Fried in lard hangs
In the kitchen. Base notes of mildew
Waft up from the basement.

Dishes dry on the sink rack.
The dripping tap
Matches the rhythm
Of the Kitty-Cat Clock
Tail swinging to and fro
Over the stove.

If People Were Trees

When a tree is old or distressed a mushroom-like growth
steps up the trunk, the fungus a sign of something
else gathering inside. This secret dying called heart-rot
afflicts the tree with a moist and spongy center
but to look at it, you wouldn't know except
for the tell-tale fungus below. If people
were trees we could see the blight
climbing up to their knees. With people
you must press a finger into their lower limbs
to feel the fluid hidden within. People and trees
are expert at walling off decay to spare the living parts.
This is only a fleeting fix. Each day
it will get bigger, the thing in the middle.

Grandma's Letters—Our Soldiers Fought Them

*You know I keep wondering what our government is going to do
with all of these refugees. There is no work to be had for our own
people, yet they talk of putting newcomers to work. For 10 years
our soldiers fought them and now suddenly, they are moving in.
I just don't understand politics, I guess.*

Her only son killed
In World War II
Lies in French soil.
A new war, new foes

From Vietnam take jobs
No one wants at the gypsum plant,
Change the color of the town.

Hopeless Entanglement

The top two drawers of Mom's dresser
are all I have left to empty, find a home for,
breathe in the Miss Dior that clings
to contents that refuse to be separated
and sorted into piles. Each lower drawer
was stuffed—here gloves, there worn-out panties,
bras (all white), hankies, slips, pajama tops
(no bottoms?) When Mom's family visited,
she and her sisters always found their way
to her bedroom. Mom pulled out her costume
jewelry and they sat on the bed, gossiped,
and tried on necklaces or cocktail rings.
The aunt who made us laugh al¬ways cooed,
Can I have this? Please? for anything new.
My quiet, kind aunt usually tackled
a jumbled mass of chains with a safety pin
to tease out the knots. My cousin and I sat
cross-legged on the rug, stringing yards
of navy and pink pop-it beads.
The first drawer I open now is full of pendants,
lockets and chunky chains. Some of my Grandma
is mixed in there too in her Bakelite bracelets,
rhinestone pins, strands of fake pearls
some as small as sesame seeds.
In the final drawer, Mom's collection of cheap beads
and chains are held together by plastic shower curtain
rings that bar them from hopeless entanglement.
As I click and unclick the rings, I see my Mom's hand
setting one drawer right, kept together, safe.

Grandma's Letters—By the Sink

I sure think you chose wisely when you bought your car. I hope you can drive over to Fort Dodge and see me some time soon. Nobody ever comes to visit me. The only time the kids come over is if I ask them to come and they are reluctant sometimes even then.

Sunday afternoons
She eats alone
By the sink.

In my dreams, we all sit
Around her empty
Queen Ann table
Draped in crocheted lace.

Lysianthus Hospice

Sister blossoms in a bouquet long past
its prime, even slime in the vase
does not daunt their promise.
Pristine cream heads
almost rose-like in petal complexity
stand aloft, hover over putrid water.
Given a fresh cut, clear drink, they raise
their heads anew and open
down to the smallest bud.

A Sign We Have More Time

A TV with the volume low provides some distraction,
the ping-ping-ping signaling a game show win.
When the lunch tray arrives, I jump up desperate
for something to do—helpless waiting is the lot
of those who aren't dying. My mother-in-law wakes
surprised I am there, forgetting we hugged
and spoke only minutes ago.
I open the napkin, fuss with lids and straw.
She mutters *Yuck* at the lasagna, shakes her head.
I offer up soup, cottage cheese, a dinner roll, all *No*.
Only the diced peaches remain. I shake the container
tempting her with a smile. Like a baby bird,
she opens her mouth waiting to be fed. Spooning
her peaches, I wait for her to swallow, then ask *Ready?*
She opens her mouth in reply, each bite shattering my heart.
With the last bit of syrup gone, she murmurs, *More peaches.*
I rush out of her room to get what she wants.
Surely, this is a sign we have more time.
I search both kitchens in the hospice. No peaches.
I start to panic then see an untouched tray outside
another patient's door. Not caring why this stranger didn't eat,
I snatch the peaches. When I get back, she is asleep again.
I catch my breath, whisper questions to Jeopardy answers,
standing ready when she wakes with my prize and a spoon.

Ode to a Wild Turkey Hen

By the rear windows of our study
you scrutinize your reflection,
bob your bumpy blue head and softly gobble
a greeting to the hen in the glass.

Turkeys forage in flocks but you are
always alone. Every evening when you
tour our yard, you leave tracks on top
of your own tracks in the snow.

You are careful of your toilette,
grooming the feathers on your tail
and breast, tarnished silver muted
with copper and green—the intricate design

meant to meld with dead leaves and bark,
camouflage from fox or dog. You cock
your head and turn a shiny black eye
rimmed in red. So close are we

I see the frigid air stir your wispy eyelashes.
I admire your stately gait, claws curl then
unfurl with each slow step. You pause
on our front porch before you launch

into clumsy flight to roost in the rafter
of the elms across the road, settling
your wings, safe for the night.

Grandma's Letters—Far from the Library

I wish I were not so far from the library. Years ago I got books from them. It seems a shame to buy books because once they are read, I am stuck with them. I gave a bunch to the library not long ago. The librarian came and got them and was tickled to get them. Not only that, but he gave me a write-up in the paper.

Dependent on rides
For essentials like groceries
And heart pills,
Books became luxuries.

Explains why so many books
On her shelves
Were Reader's Digest Condensed.

The Road to Alzheimer's

He first noticed misplaced words,
streets changing direction,
then the symptoms hardened.
Not the greatest sorrow to bear,
that was yet to come.
Now, whenever the garage door
opens, the creak of the springs
awakens the betrayal anew.
His pale blue eyes
sharpen, pierce through
tears as rage reddens his neck.
He rails at his wife.
She shrinks inside her coat,
braces herself as he drives
in the roundabout of his mind.
Nothing will detour the rant.
How could you take my keys?
Forbid me to drive my car?
a thousand times over.
A slight he cannot forget.

Grandma's Letters—On My Bended Knees

*I suppose I had better tell you why I was sick; well it happened
this way. I was in my own bedroom, down on my <u>bended knees</u>—
not praying as you might assume but getting something from a
dresser drawer when I lost my balance and fell flat on my butt. I
think tail bone is the word and I think fracture is the word to best
describe it and I think hurt is another word.*

I think fear
Is the word. Better not
Tell us, to check
Our worry for her.

Losing balance first of all
A warning sign.

How I Remember Her

I paddle about in my dreams
before they evaporate, grasping
at flotsam to keep me in the world
of sleep. I clutch
a piece of dream wreckage—
a dusty station wagon
rumbling by, full of children,
sweaty grown-ups
all strangers save my Grandma.
She waves, says, "Hi, honey.
How are you?" I am so happy,
long to reply, but I wake
before I can tell her.

Coin Laundromat

The shushing of suds and socks,
comfort of a cycle, predictable
and timed, scent of lavender, blend
of bleach, the hum and warmth of dryers
create a sanctuary where strangers offer
quarters to fill the last slot, become
intimates folding underwear, or restore
an errant baby sock to its owner.
People sit and text, watch the cars pass by,
or gaze as their clothes fall forward
then back. A place where folks
seek refuge from the weather, bicker
with their demons, or just use
the toilet. Everyone bathes
in the fluorescent, flickering lights—
a spiritual cleansing.

The Television Talks to Me

After five days in the ICU, my elderly mother was weaned off the ventilator. Groggy but aware, she tried to speak in a raspy voice. I couldn't understand her. She raised a finger to me, a sign to wait. She opened her mouth and started pulling the crud from the roof of her mouth that collects there when a patient is on a vent. It looked like chunks of pale, pink cement. She reached for my hand, turned it palm up and plopped the slimy mess there. As I washed my hands, she cleared her throat and said, "The television talks to me." I gently explained in the way people talk to the demented that the television couldn't talk to her. "The television isn't even on now," I replied. She rolled her eyes, "I know, but when the TV is on, a man, maybe a reporter, calls me by name. I think he wants to interview me." When I left at the end of the day, I asked the nurses to watch her for symptoms of confusion. I worried there might be more wrong than too many days in the ICU. The next morning, I was there early for rounds. The team stood by the bed. I tucked myself close to Mom's head. A screen on the wall, not the TV, bloomed into life. A physician appeared from a remote site who oversaw ICU patients for several hospitals. A great and powerful wizard, he surveyed the room, greeted the team, then addressed my mother by name. She tilted her head toward me and whispered, "See?"

Please Stand Behind this Sign to Wait

He always builds in extra time
to wait in line. Admissions,
like confession, needs space
to share secrets like date of birth
and primary insurer. He clutches
his homemade chart,
maroon and worn, to his chest.
Cradles lab reports and scans
as if they are sacred art.
Illuminated scripture writ
in radioactive gilt, all it lacks
is a ribbon to mark
the spot for today's reading
from the Book of Job. He holds
out his wrist for a paper bracelet.
Laminated number in hand,
he finds a seat among
the expectant faithful.
More than one Band-Aid
is displayed on his tissue-paper
skin. His fly zipper barely holds
his belly in. The tech shouts
a patient number,
"Oh-sixty-five." He rises,
waves his card and calls out,
"Bingo."

Third Round

I can smell the ink in a weathered issue of *People*,
the scent like charred plastic. The carpet reeks
of something sour and synthetic. My mouth brims
with saliva. I swallow hard. I look at other
patients; easy to spot—pale, no eyebrows
or lashes, faces frozen in surprise. Their healthy,
hapless companions look lost. My husband offers
soothing clichés that prickle my too thin skin.
Betrayed without and within even my marrow
conspires against me. The tech calls my name.
I lean back in a recliner, offer up my bared chest
to a large bore needle the nurse drives
into my port, an aperture
to my superior vena cava.
She uses her thumb on the roller clamp
to release the flow that goes
straight to my heart.

A Bit of Aqua Egg Shell

My walk takes me along a street
ten blocks uptown from the river
that grew the city. I pass by the hospital
where I was born, where I once worked
as a new nurse. Today, the hospital
is a nursing home. The brick wall still stands
at the edge of the property where years ago
on a summer evening a teenage patient
jumped the fence while the others played
sedated volleyball. To escape the psych unit,
he ran straight off the six-foot wall where
he seemed to hang in the air, then plummeted.
I chased him, saw him fall. My arms pinwheeled
on the edge. Breathless I looked down, relieved
he was not dead, a fractured ankle instead.
Further down the street on my walk,
sleeping stone lions rest on the stoops
of several houses. When I was small,
riding in the back of my father's Packard,
he told me the lions were there to show us
the way to the zoo. I believed in the wisdom
of such signs, thought those lucky whose
porches held this honor. Still looking for more
lions, I nearly shatter a robin's eggshell on the sidewalk.
A few doors down, plastic toys lie scattered
on a front lawn, holding the aftermath of a fierce battle
between barnyard animals, dinosaurs, and dragons.
I round the turn toward home with purple-stained
fingers from the last mulberries clinging to the trees,
a bit of aqua eggshell the size of my thumbnail
in my pocket, and the image of a victorious cow
looming over a fallen, fuchsia-winged dragon.

Amy Haddad, PhD, MSN, MFA, FAAN has educated nurses and pharmacists at Creighton University since 1988 where she also held the Dr. C.C. and Mabel L. Criss Endowed Chair in the Health Sciences. In addition, Amy served as Director of the Center for Health Policy and Ethics at Creighton University from 2005–2018 and now holds the rank of Professor Emerita. She was selected in 2001 to be part of the Pew National Fellowship Program for Carnegie Scholars, studying the impact of patient simulations on health professional learning. She has also been a pioneer in the use of poetry, creative prose and narrative writing as approaches to teaching healthcare ethics. Her poetry and short stories have been published in the *American Journal of Nursing, Janus Head, Journal of Medical Humanities, Touch, Bellevue Literary Review, Pulse, Persimmon Tree, Annals of Internal Medicine, Aji Magazine, DASH, Oberon Poetry Magazine* and the anthologies *Between the Heart Beats and Intensive Care: More Poetry and Prose by Nurses*, University of Iowa Press, Iowa City, Iowa and *Stories of Illness and Healing: Women Write Their Bodies*, Kent State University Press, Kent, Ohio. She is the 2019 recipient of the Annals of Internal Medicine poetry prize for "Families Like This" for the best poem published in the journal. She won third-place for the 2019 Kalanithi Writing Awards from Stanford University for her poem "Dark Rides." Her poetry collection, *An Otherwise Healthy Woman*, will be published by Backwaters Press, an imprint of the University of Nebraska Press in early 2022.

CPSIA information can be obtained
at www.ICGtesting.com
Printed in the USA
BVHW030516081021
618235BV00002B/151

9 781646 625703